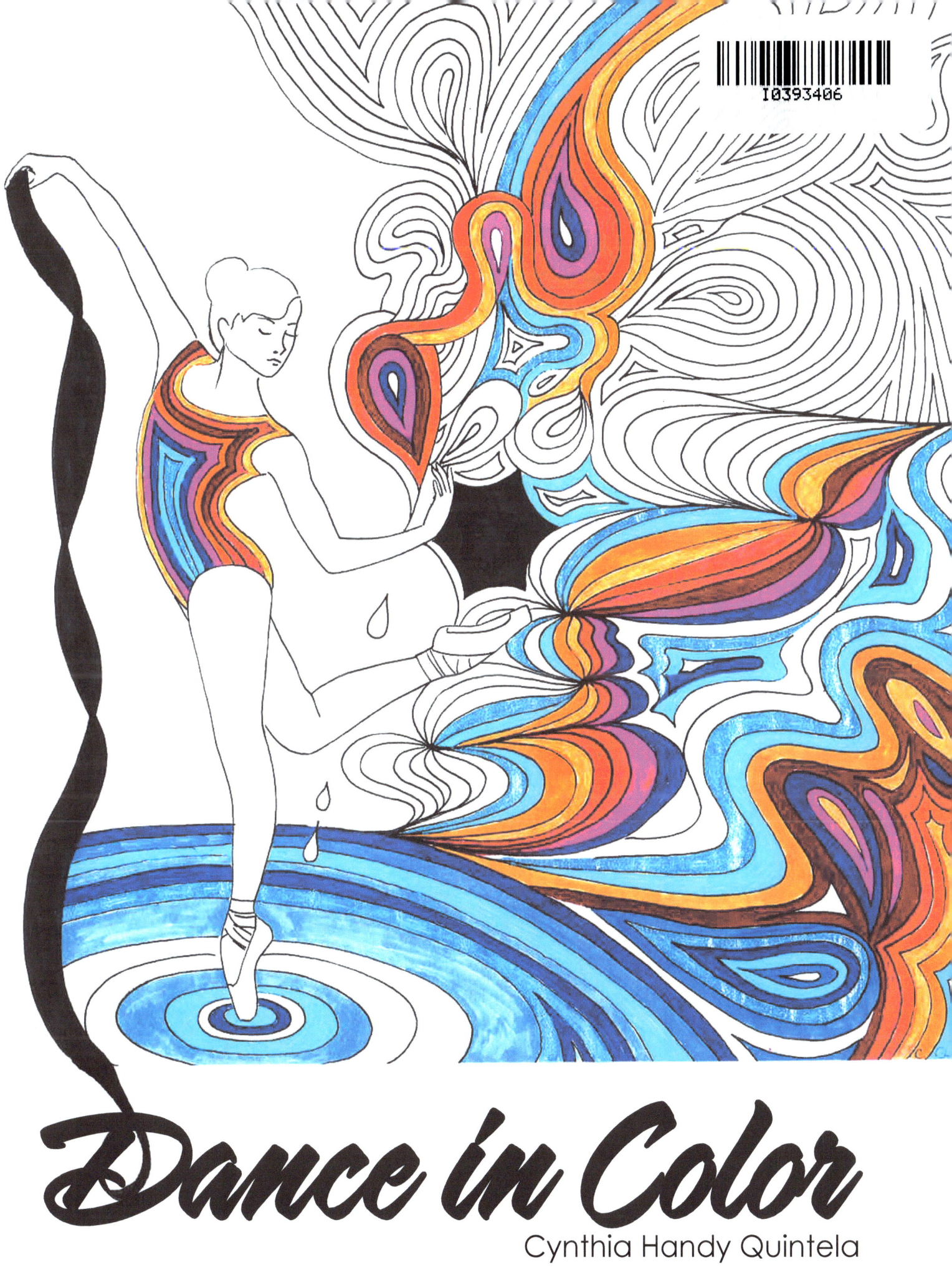

Dance in Color

Cynthia Handy Quintela

Print information available on the last page

Rev. date: 04/24/2017

To order additional copies of this book, contact:
Xlibris
1-888-795-4274
www.Xlibris.com
Orders@Xlibris.com

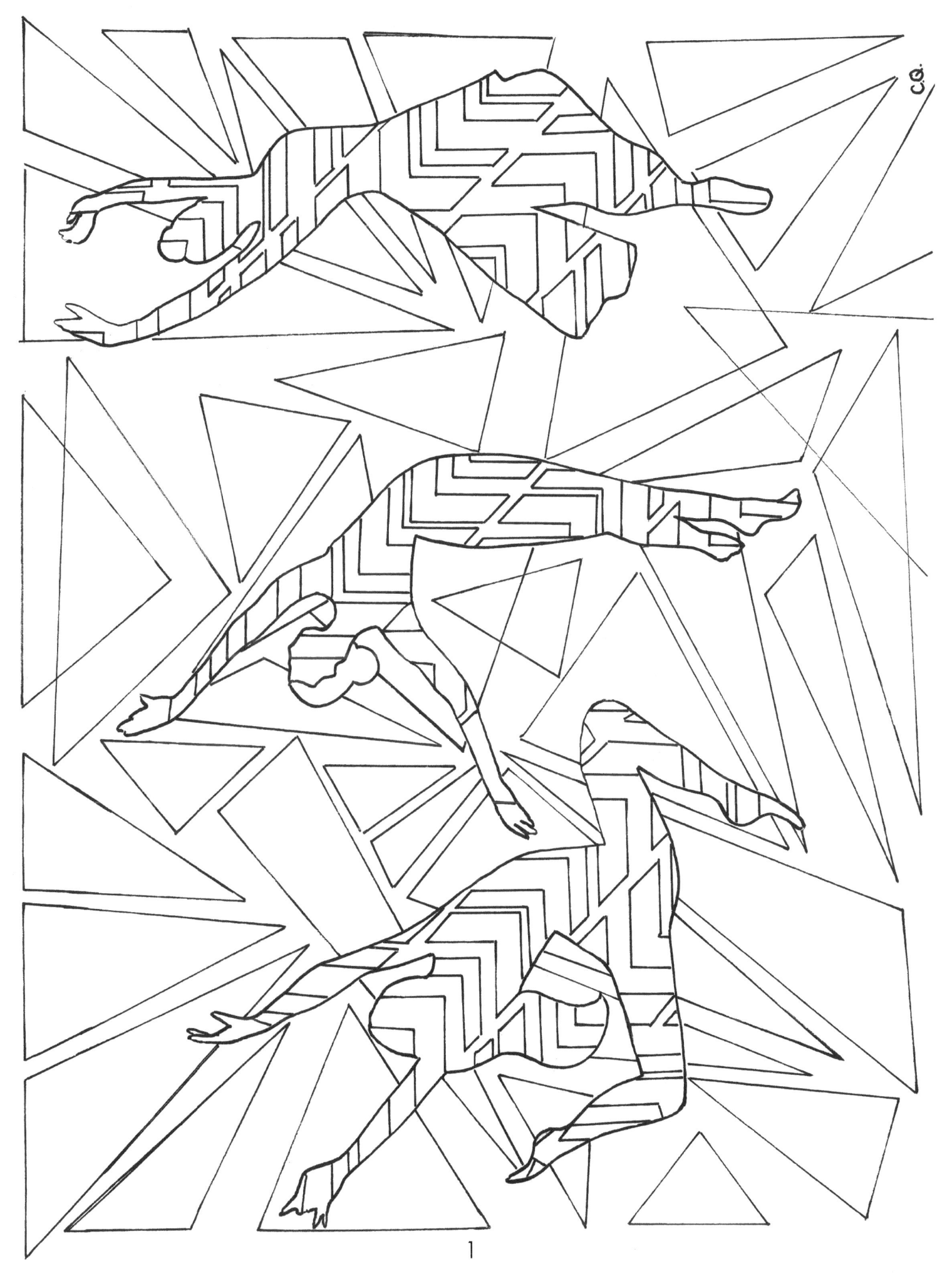

1

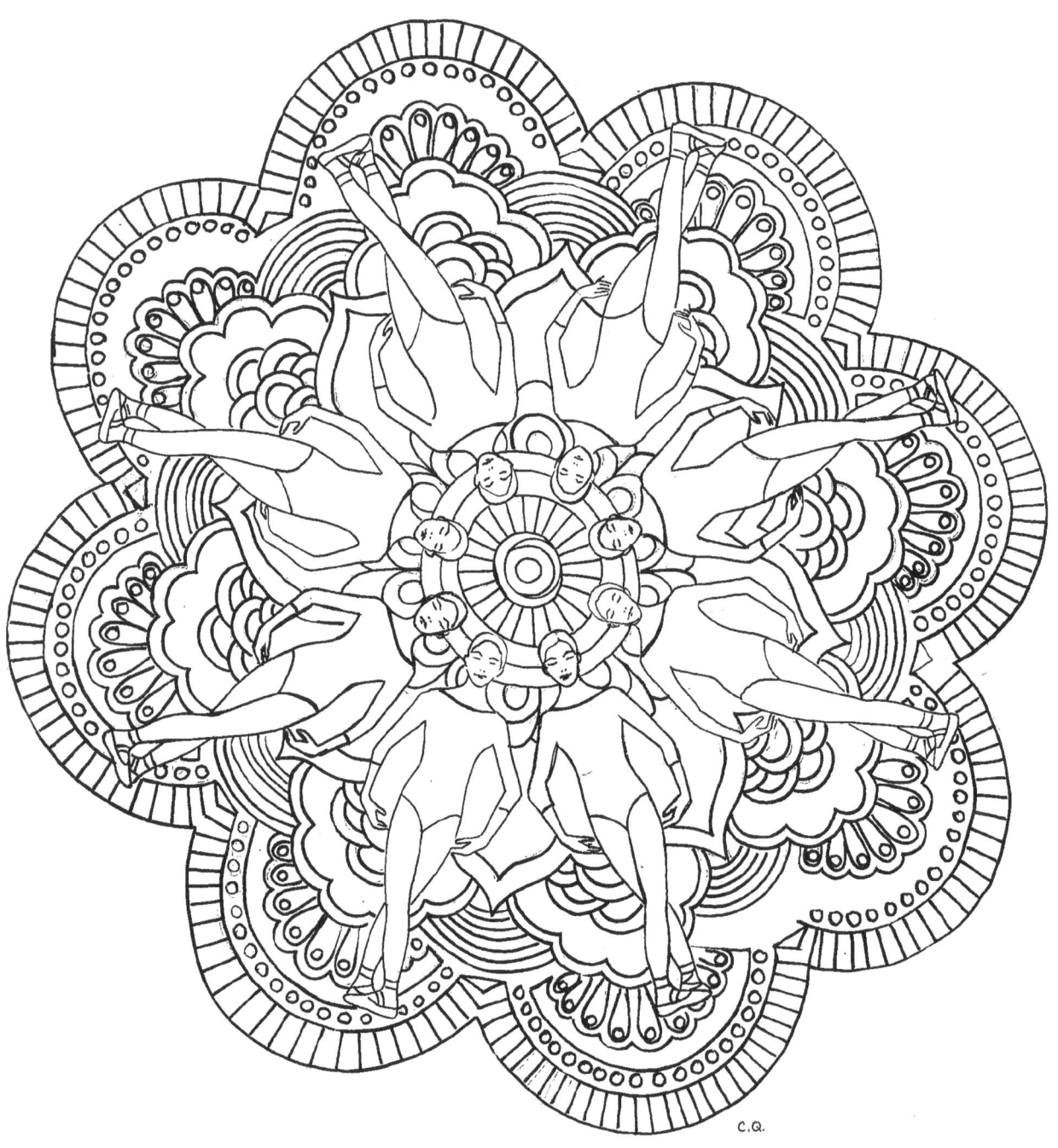

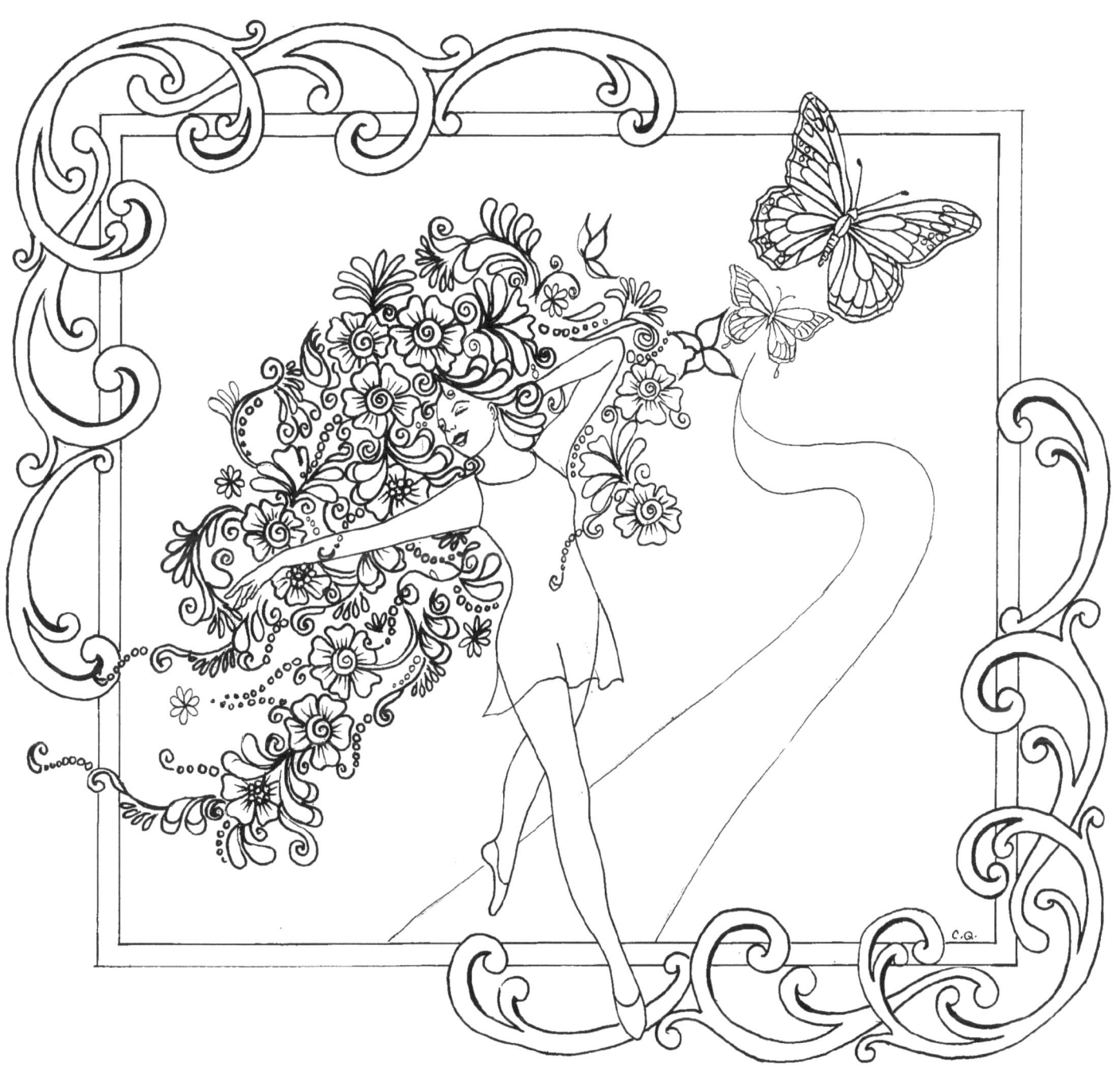

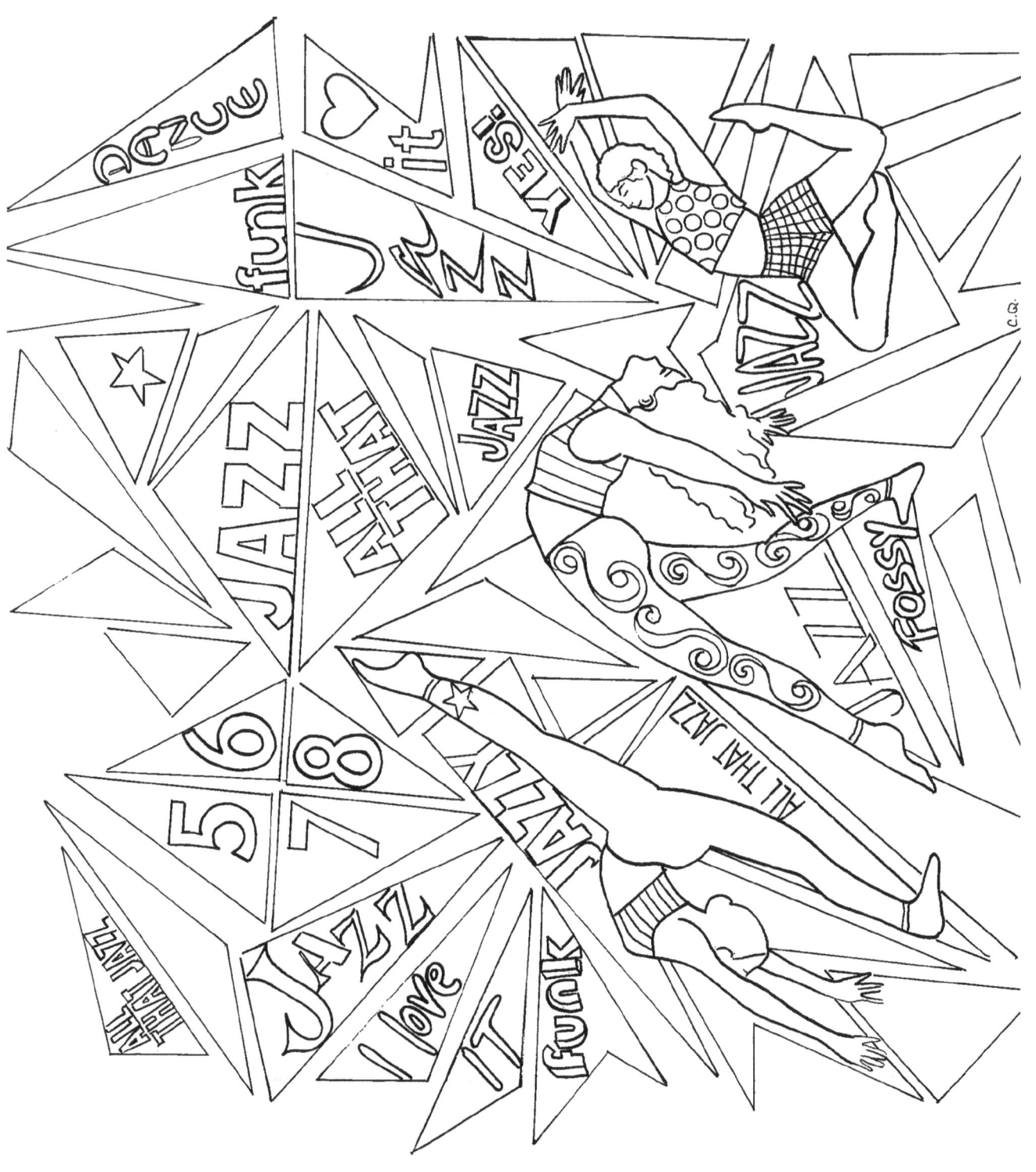

4

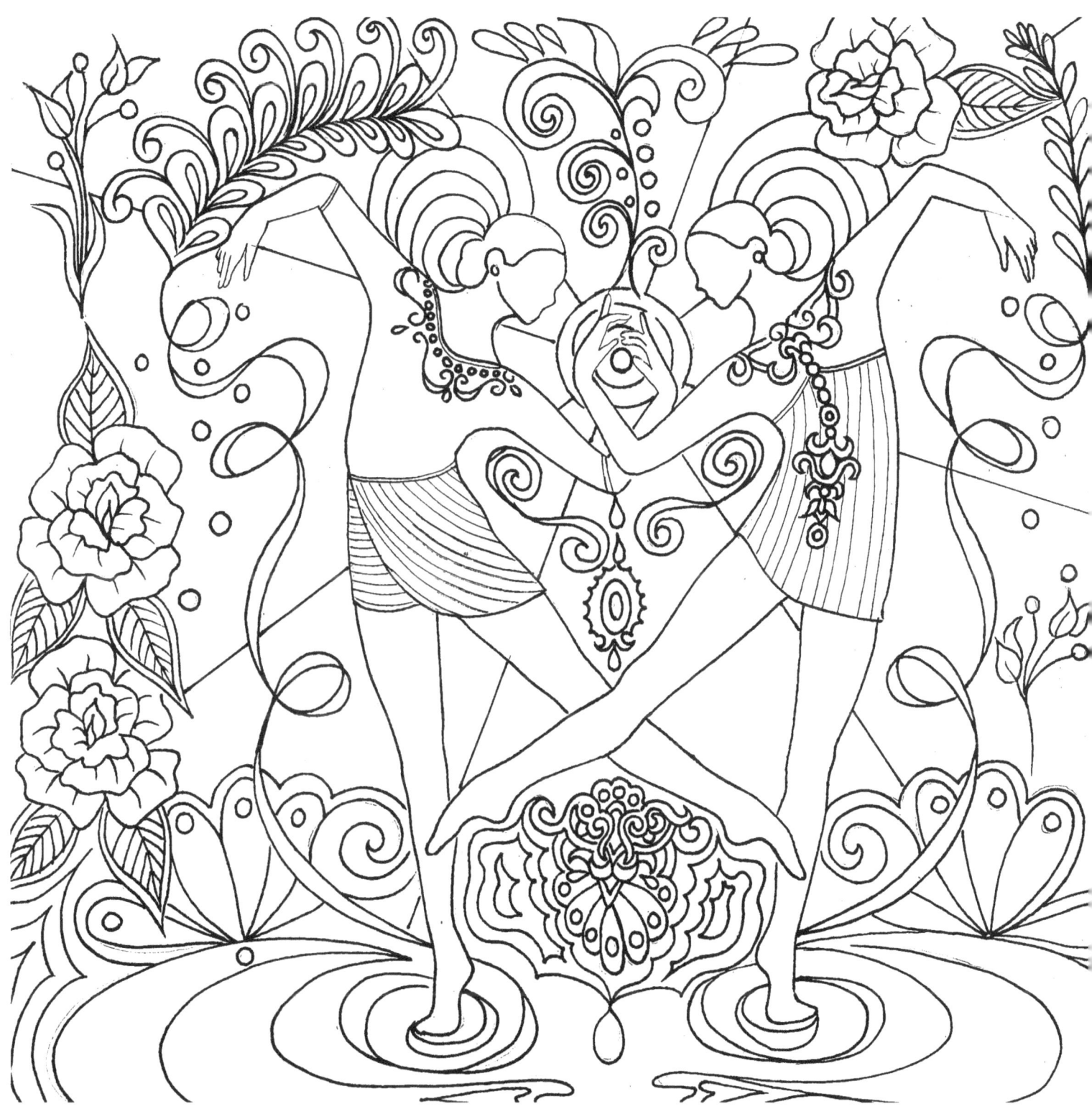

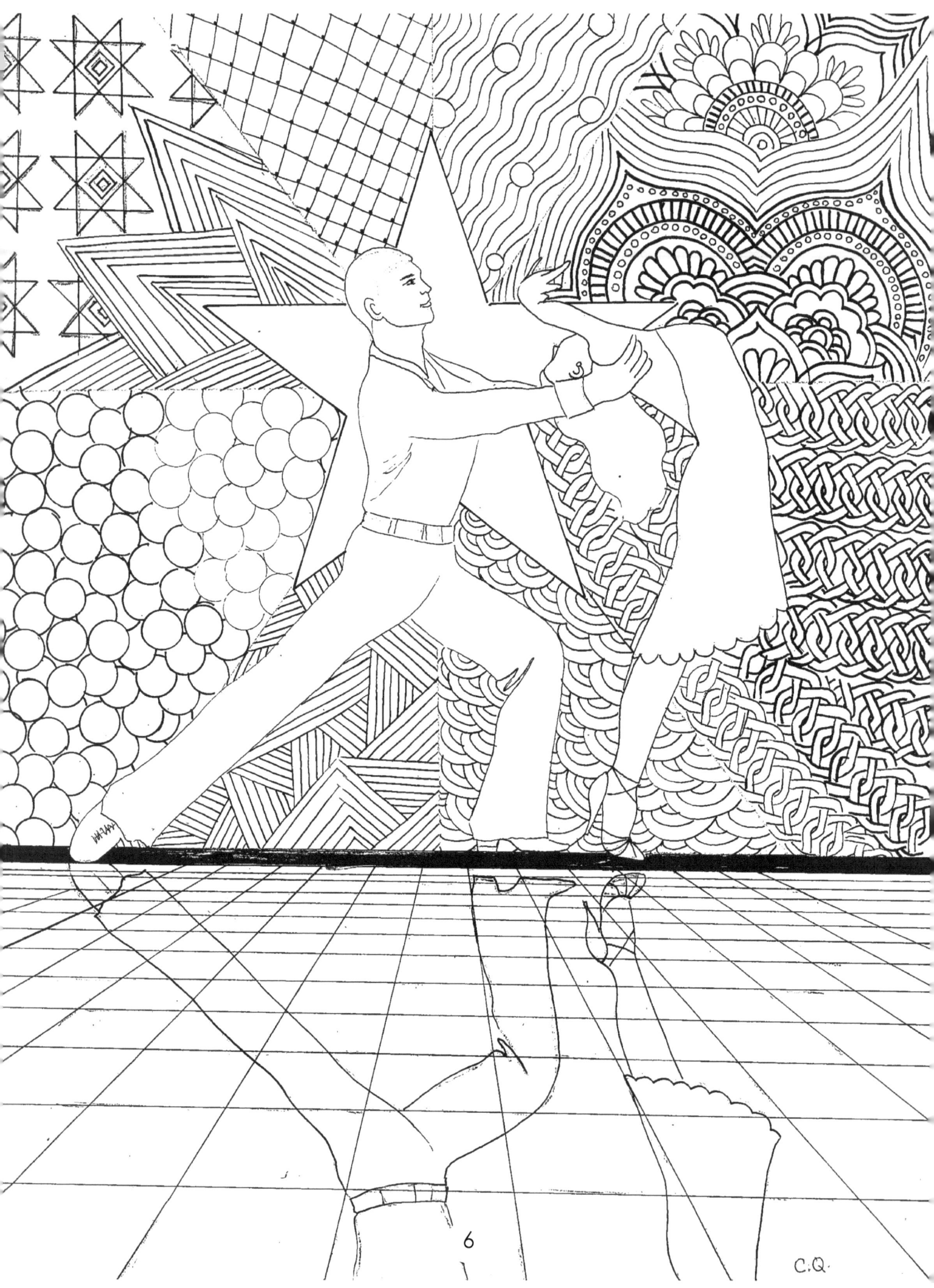

6

C.Q.

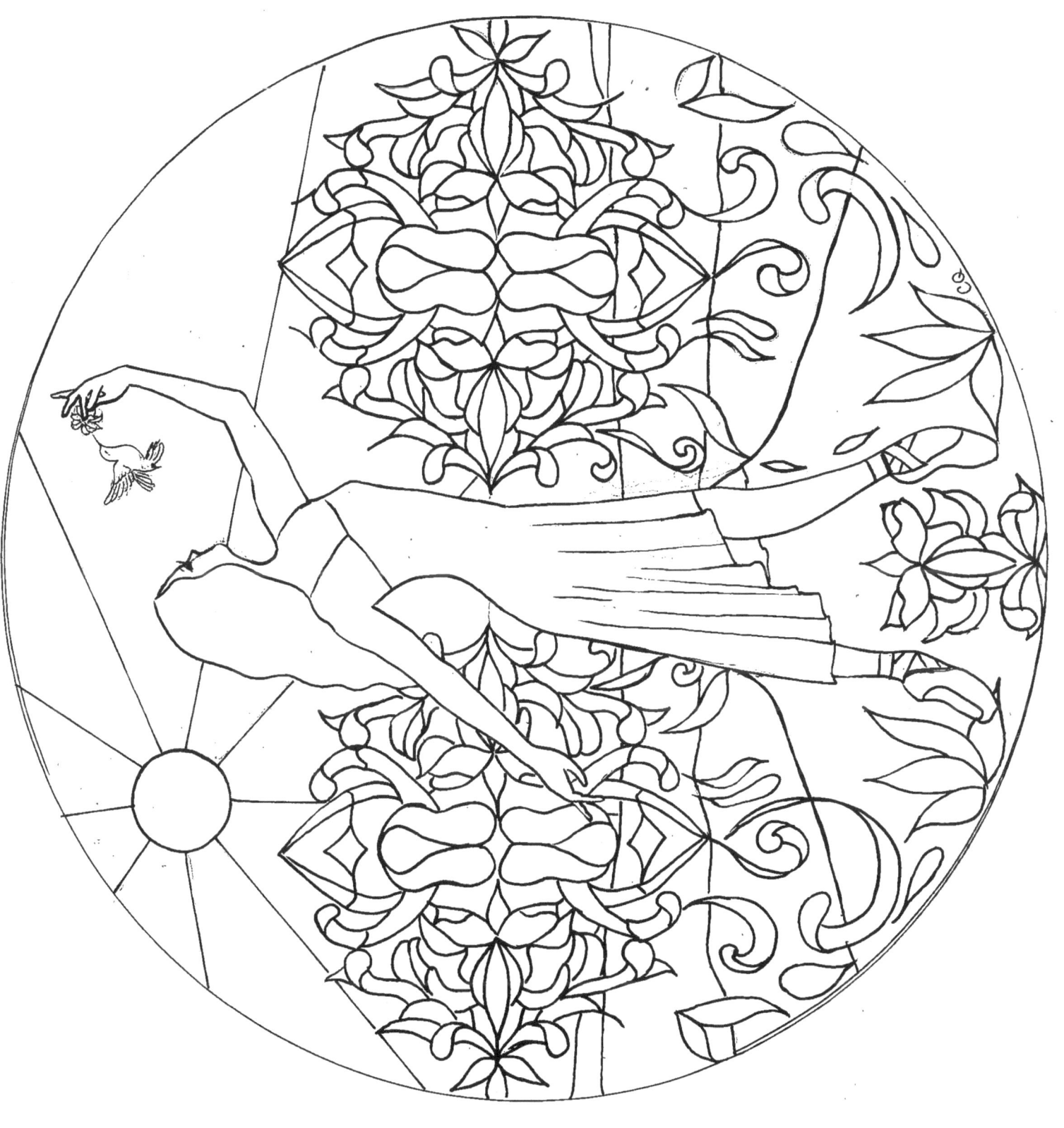

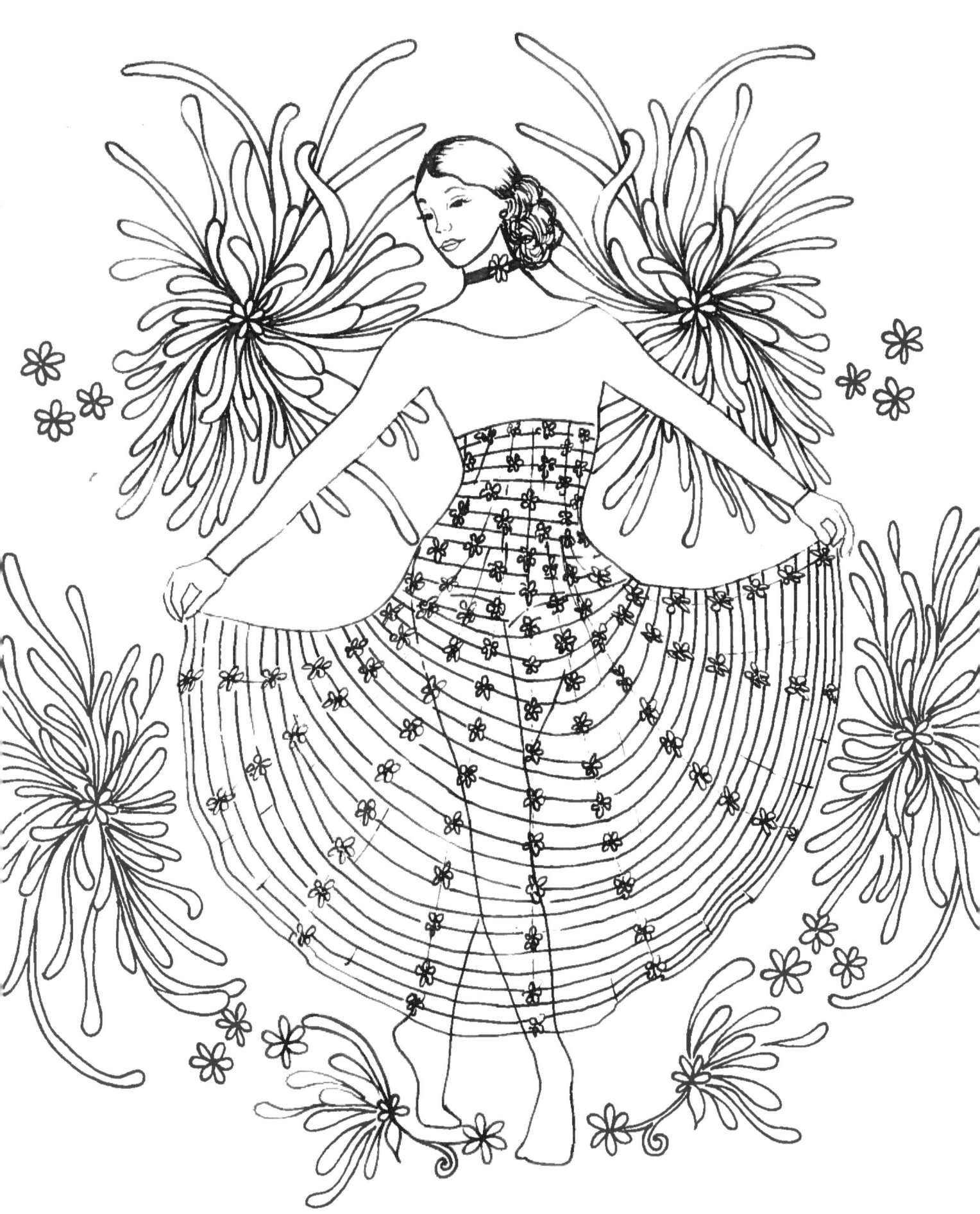

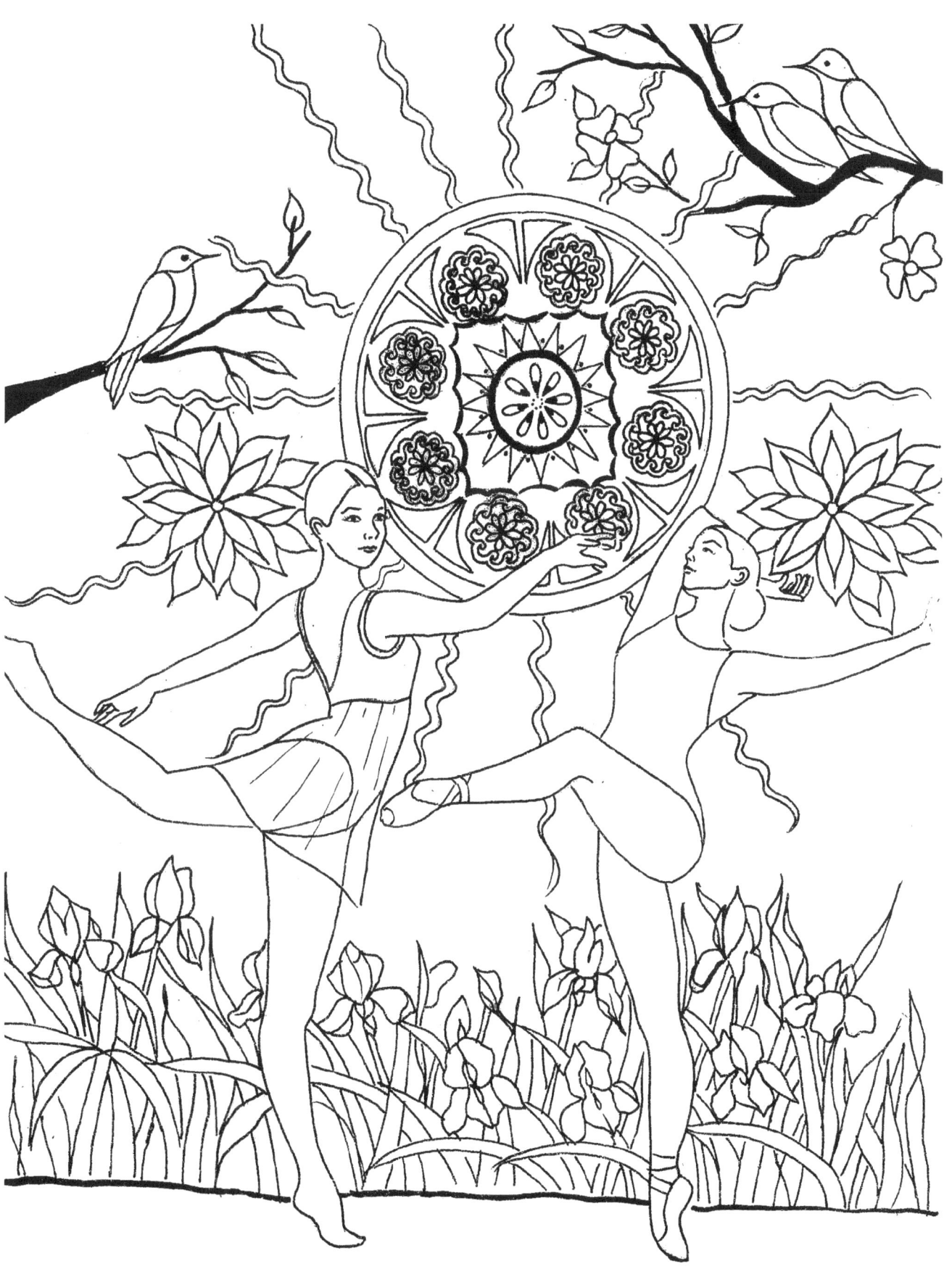

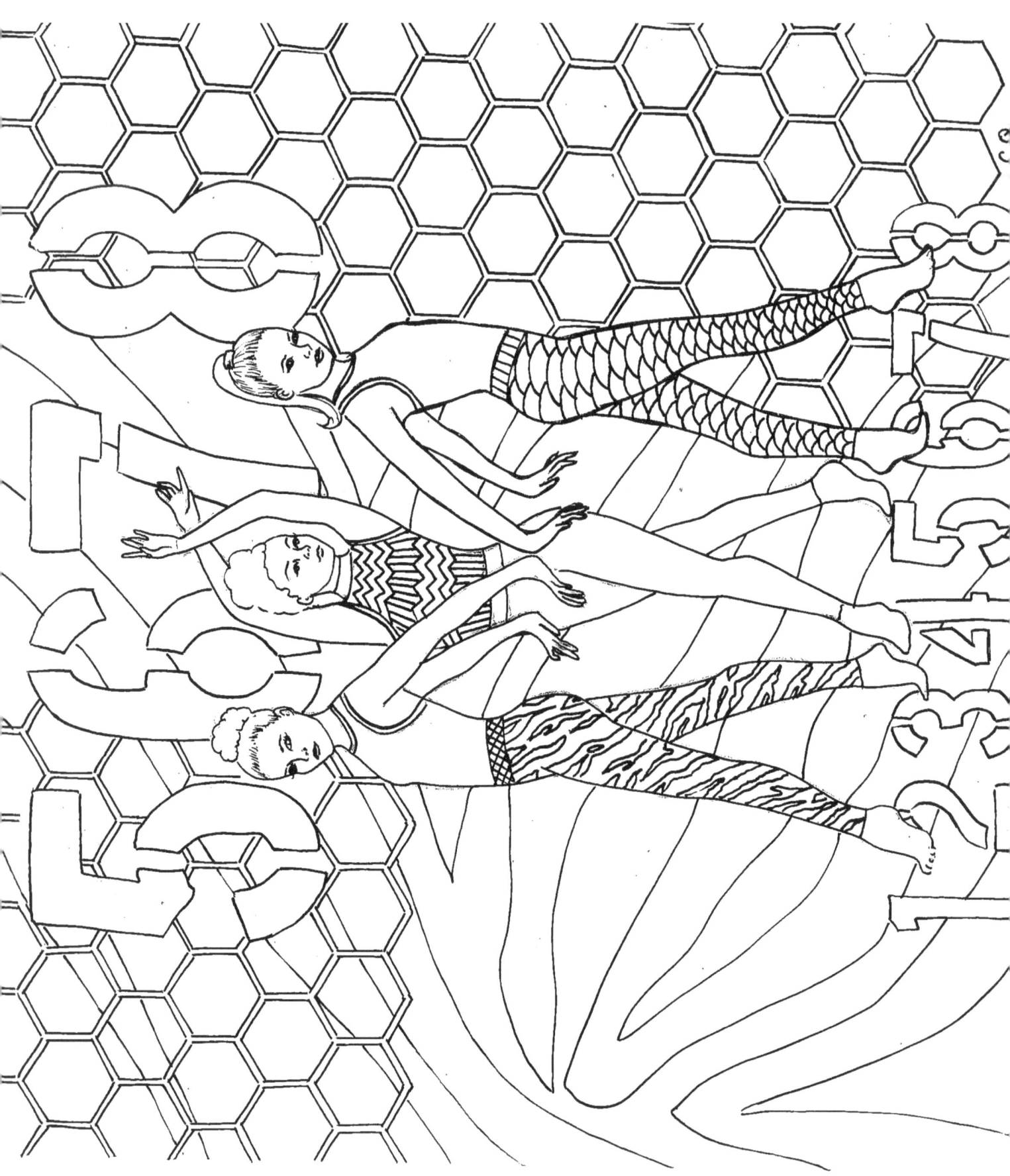

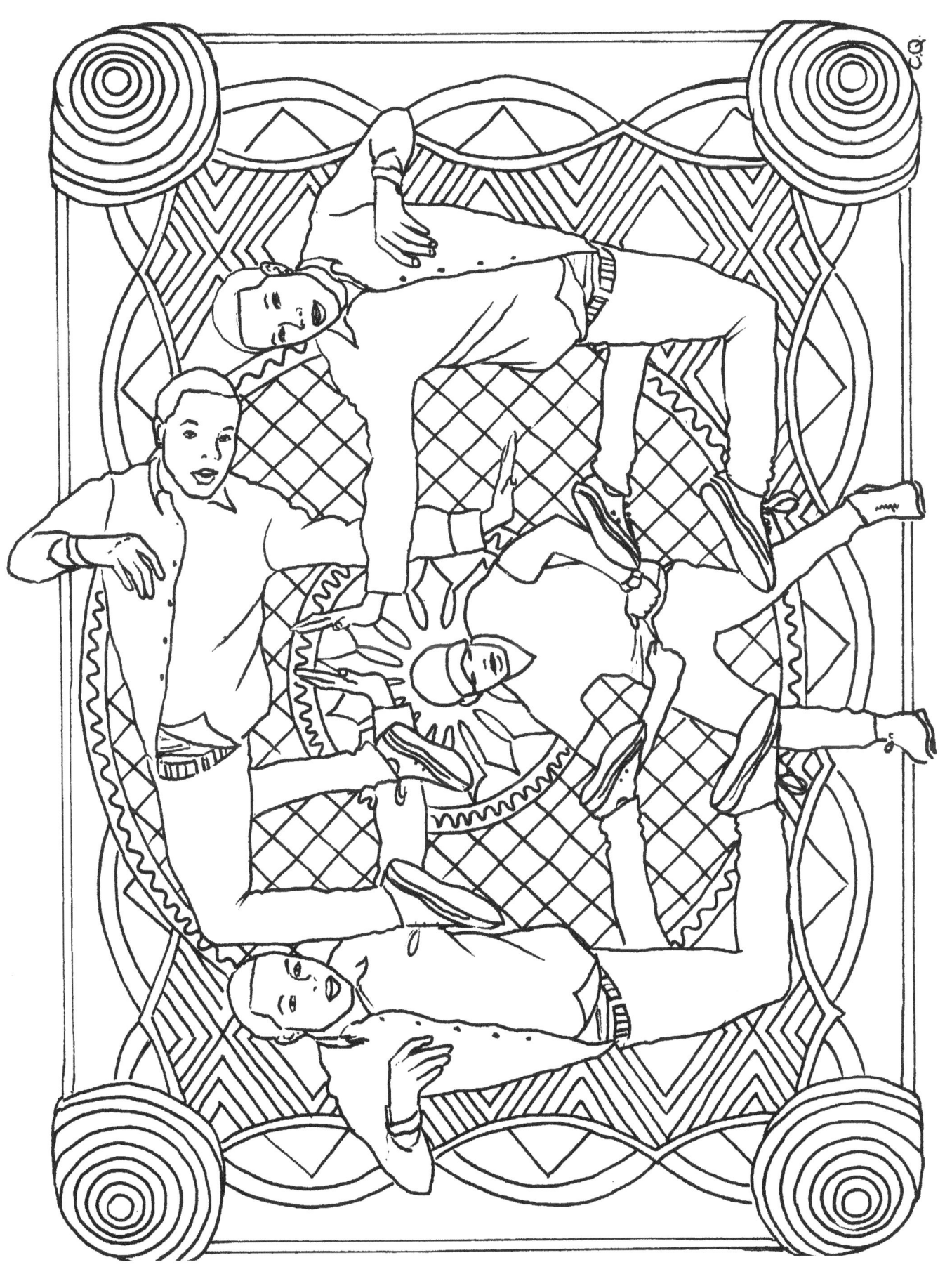

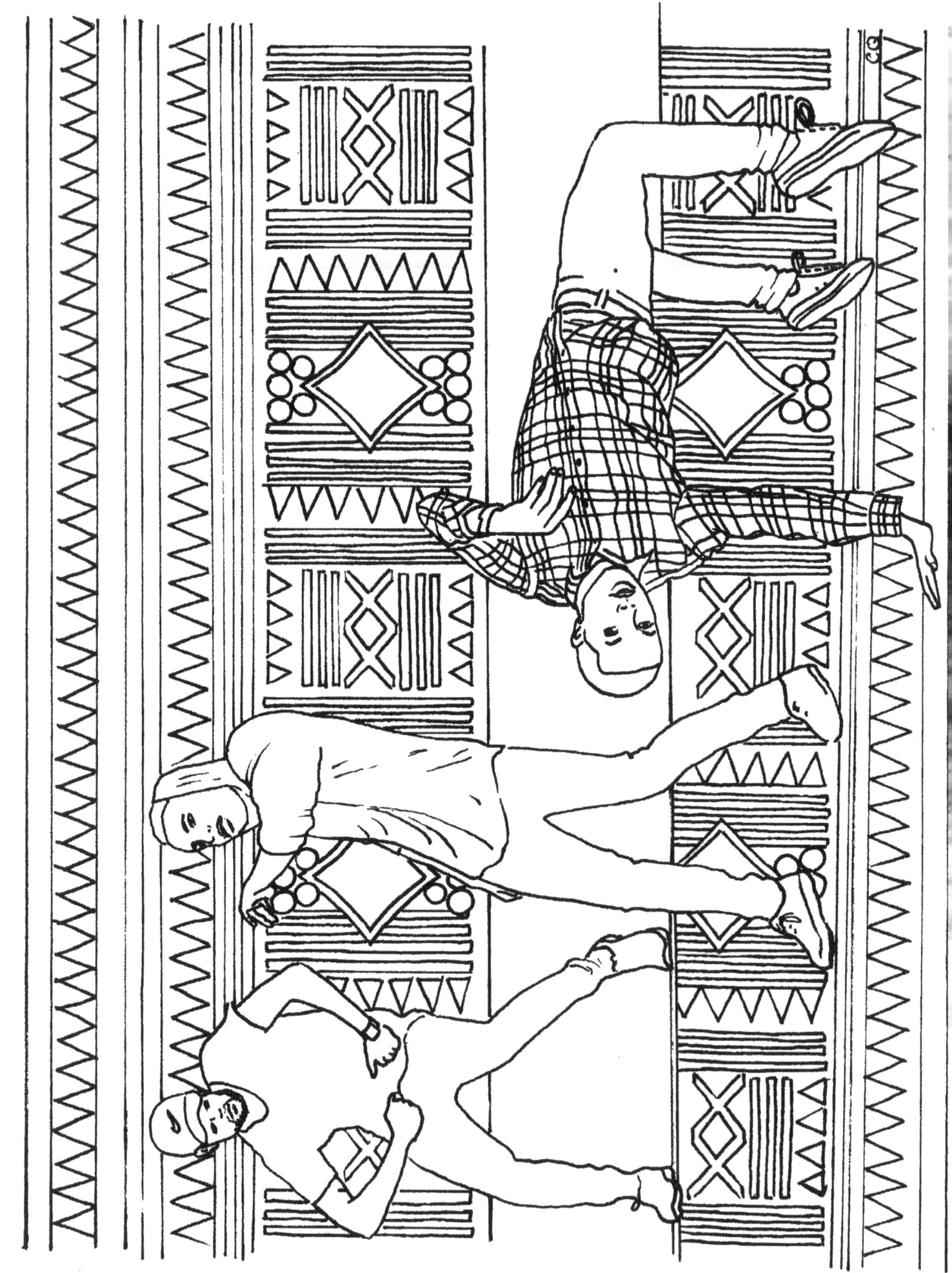

12

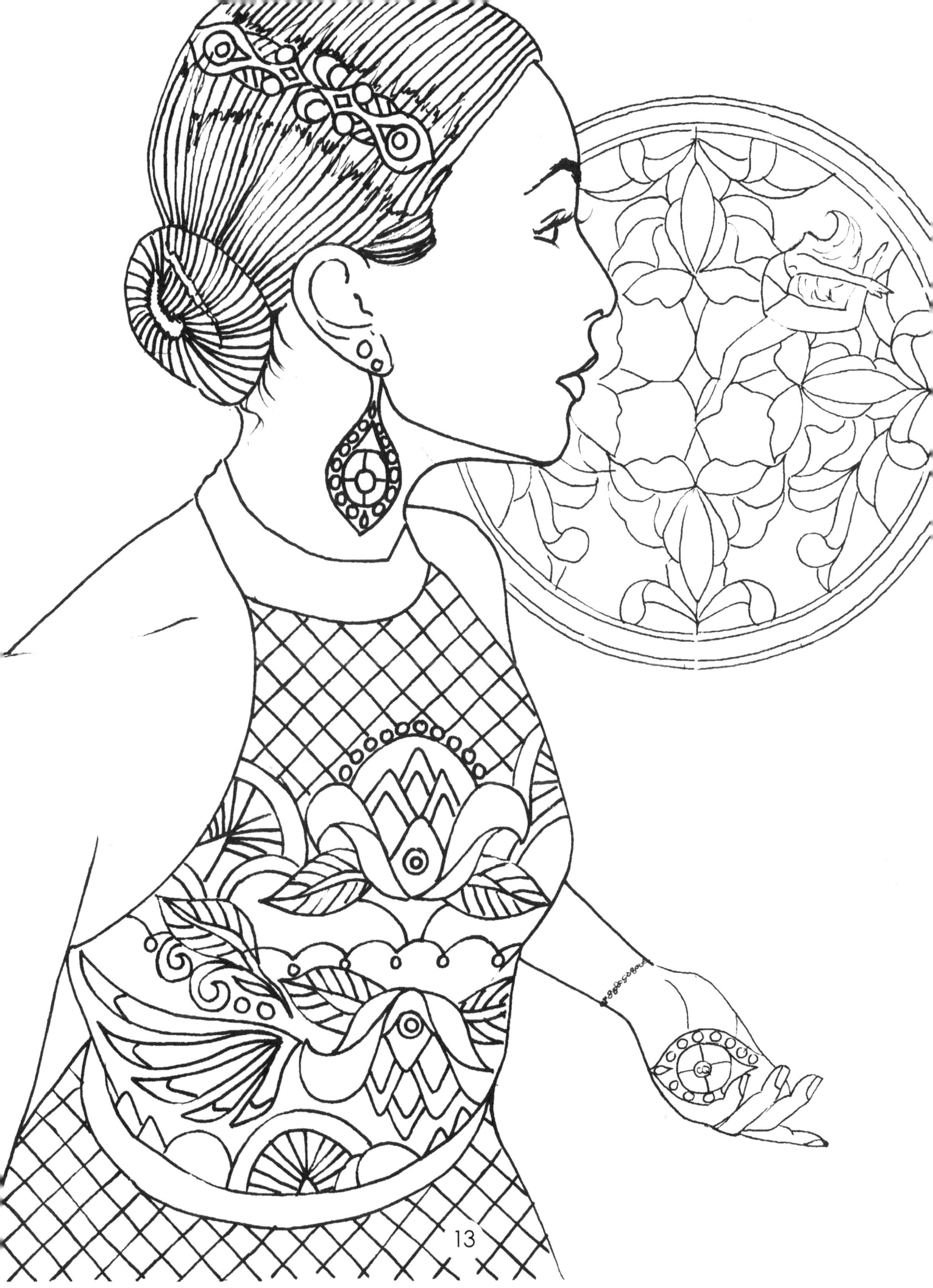

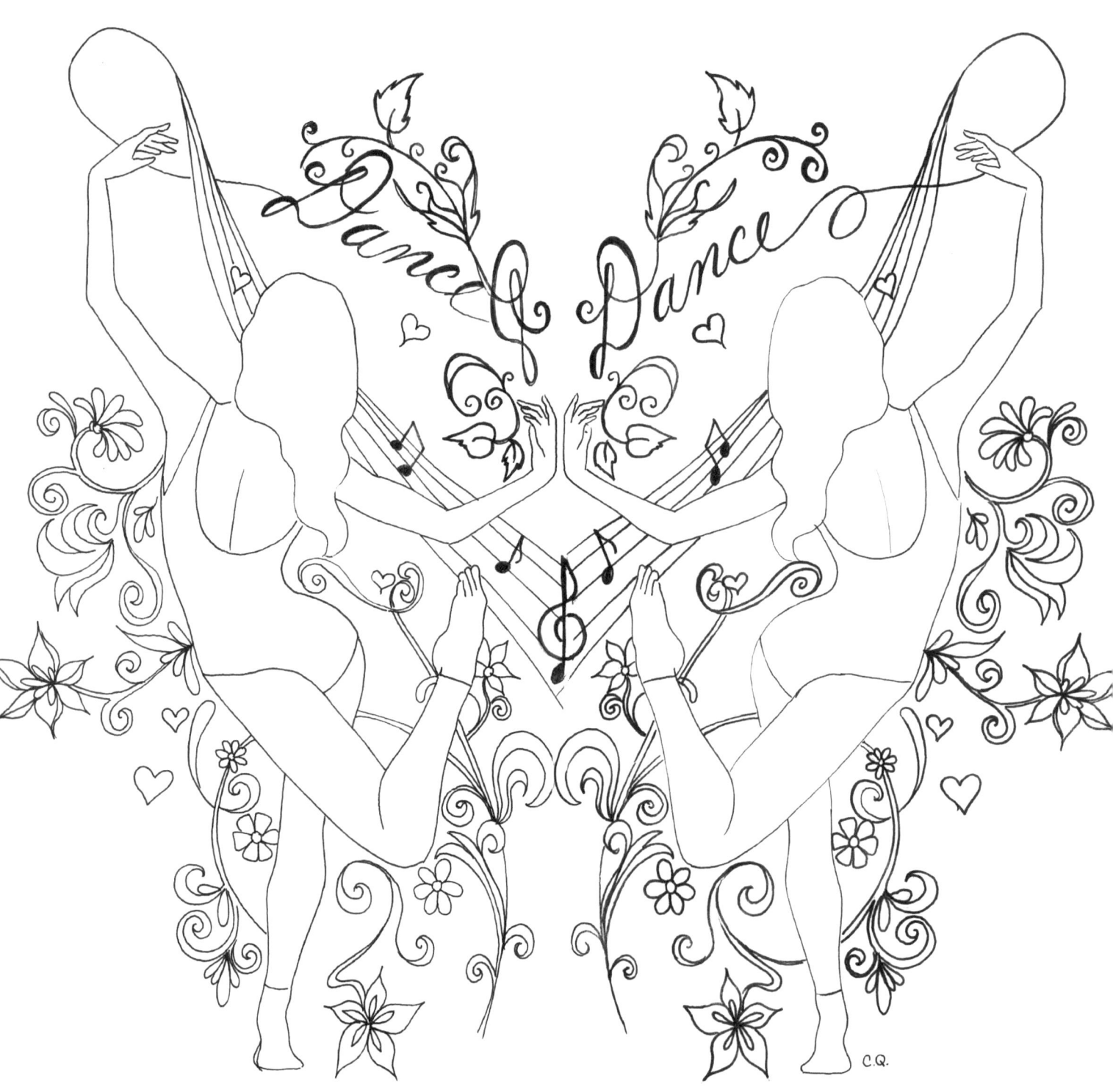

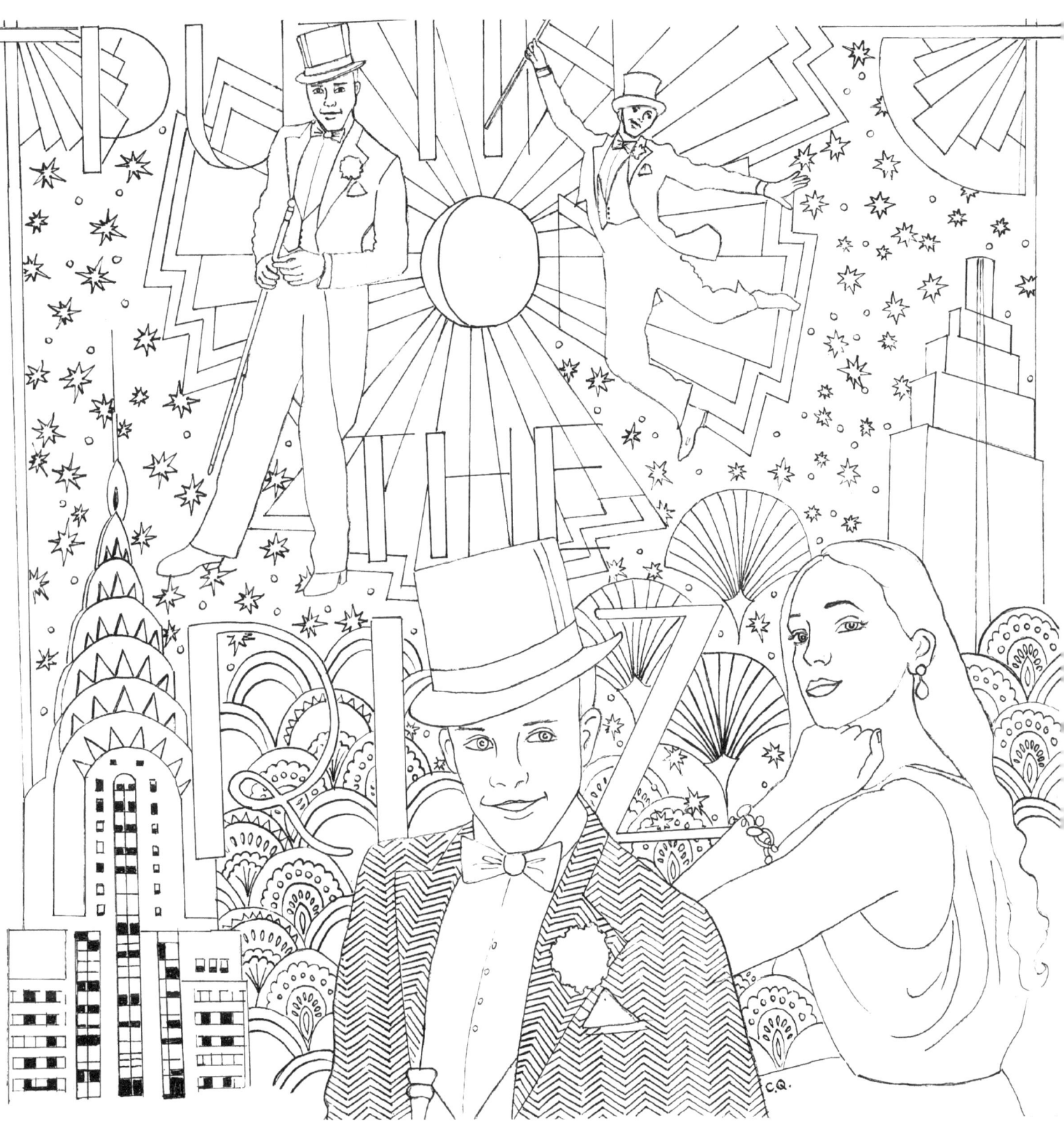

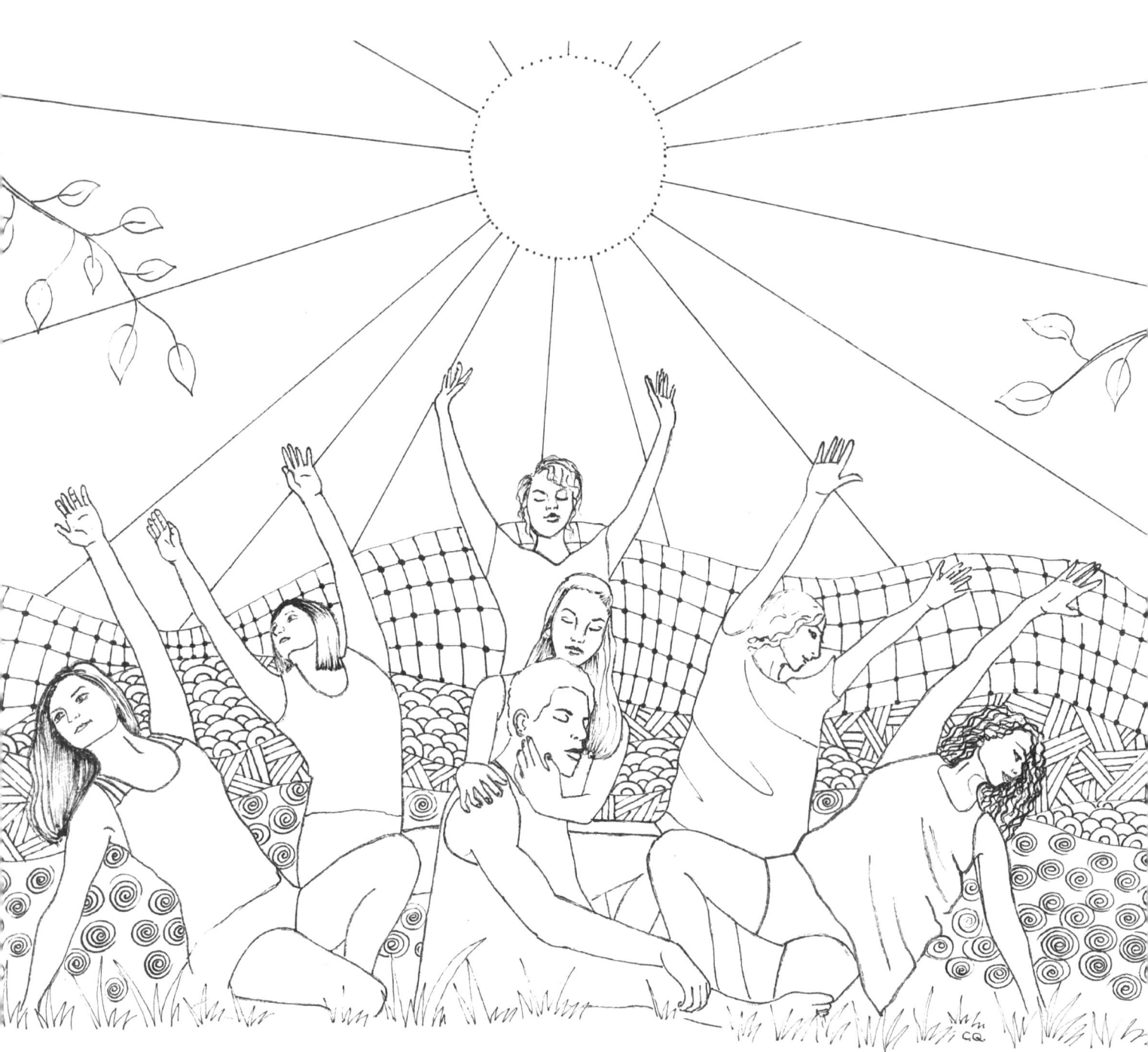

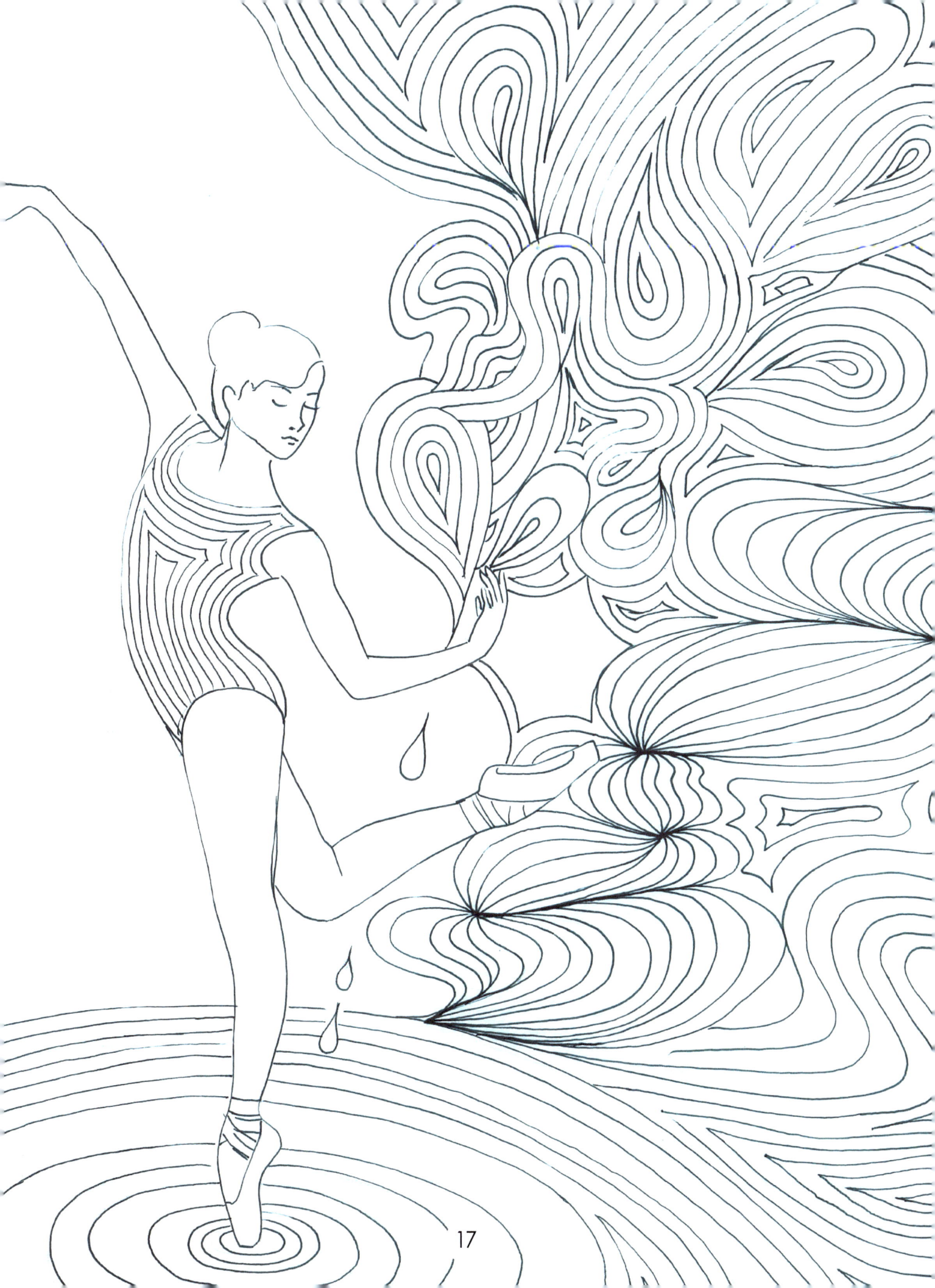

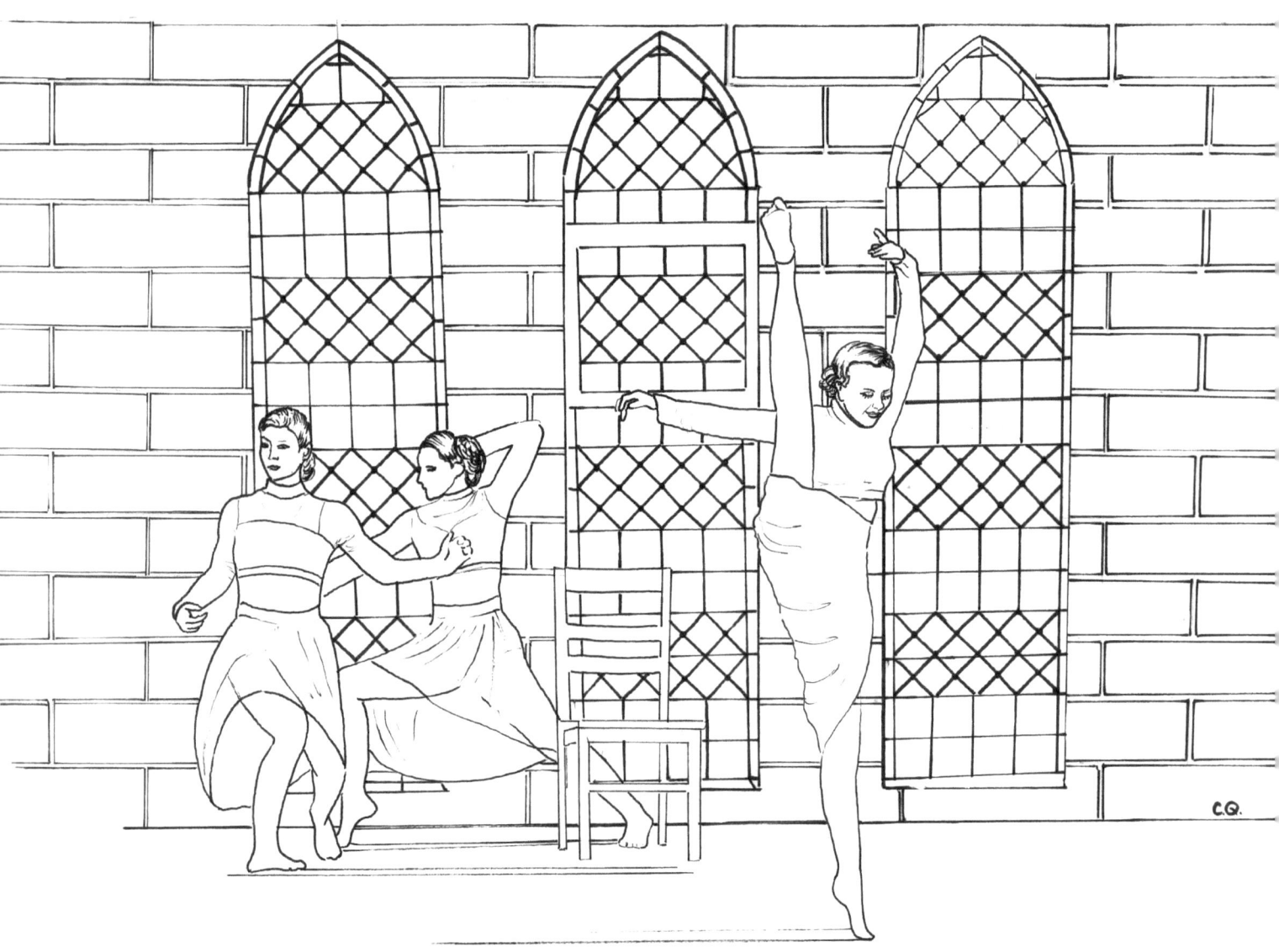

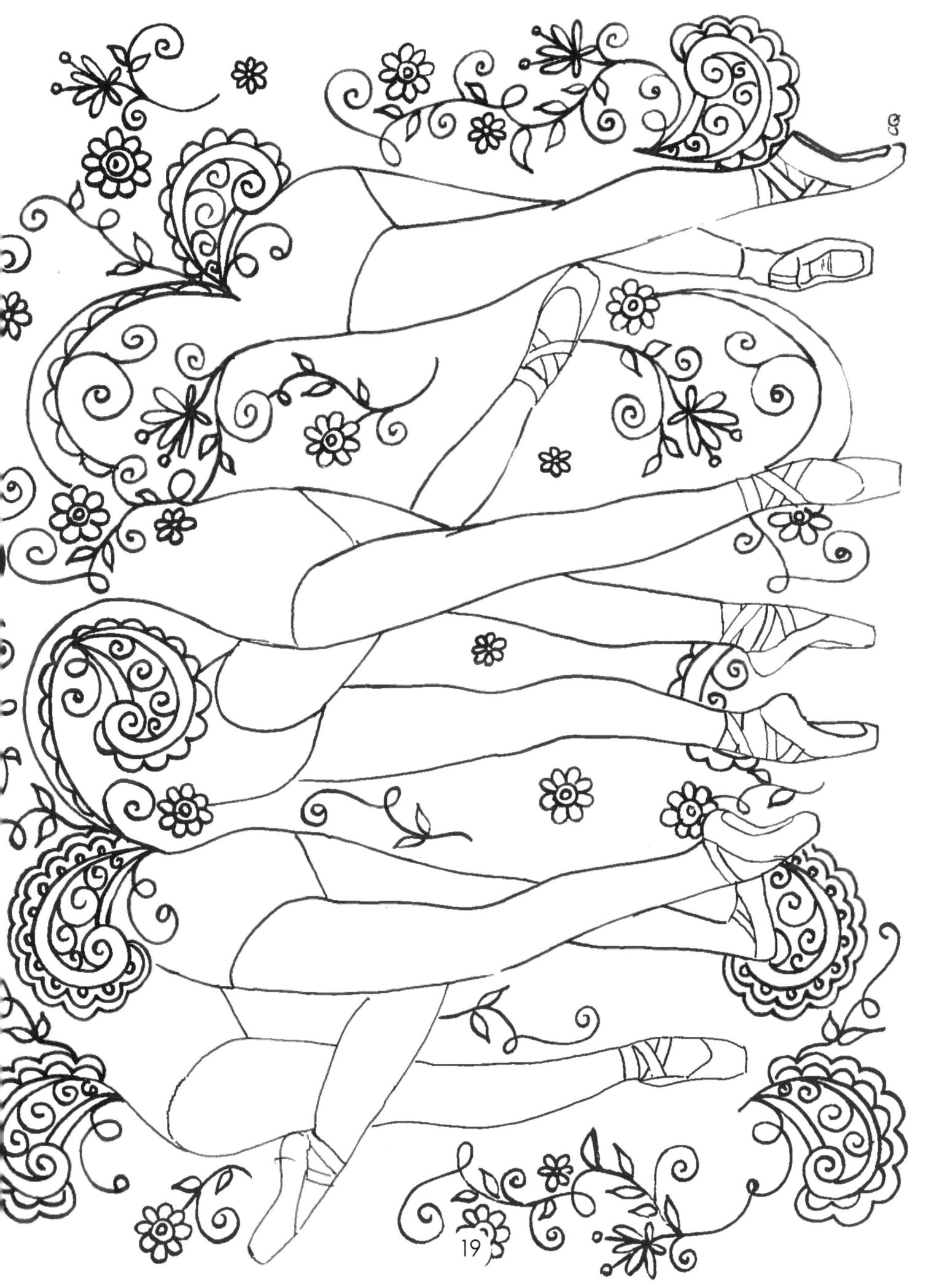

19

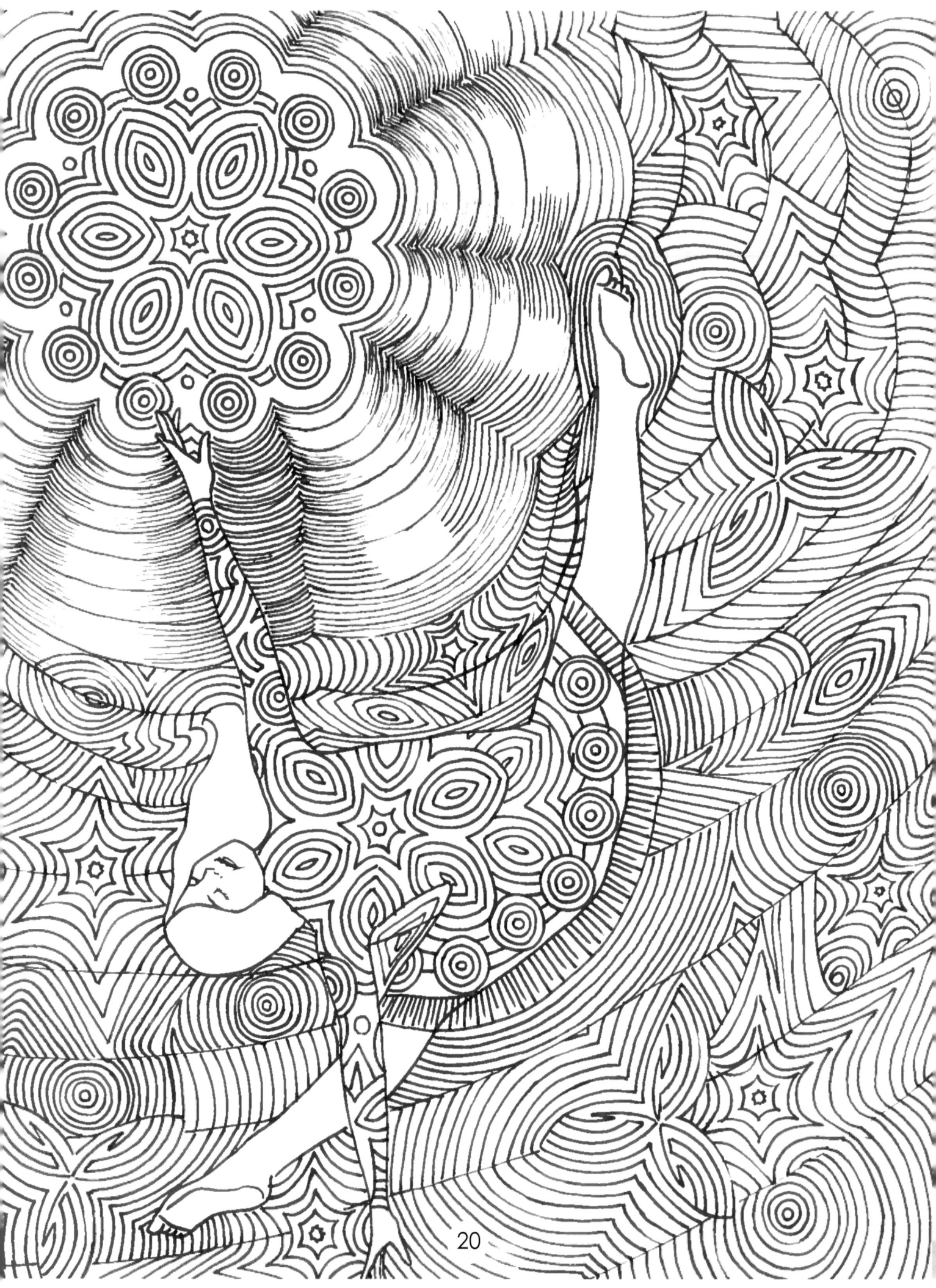

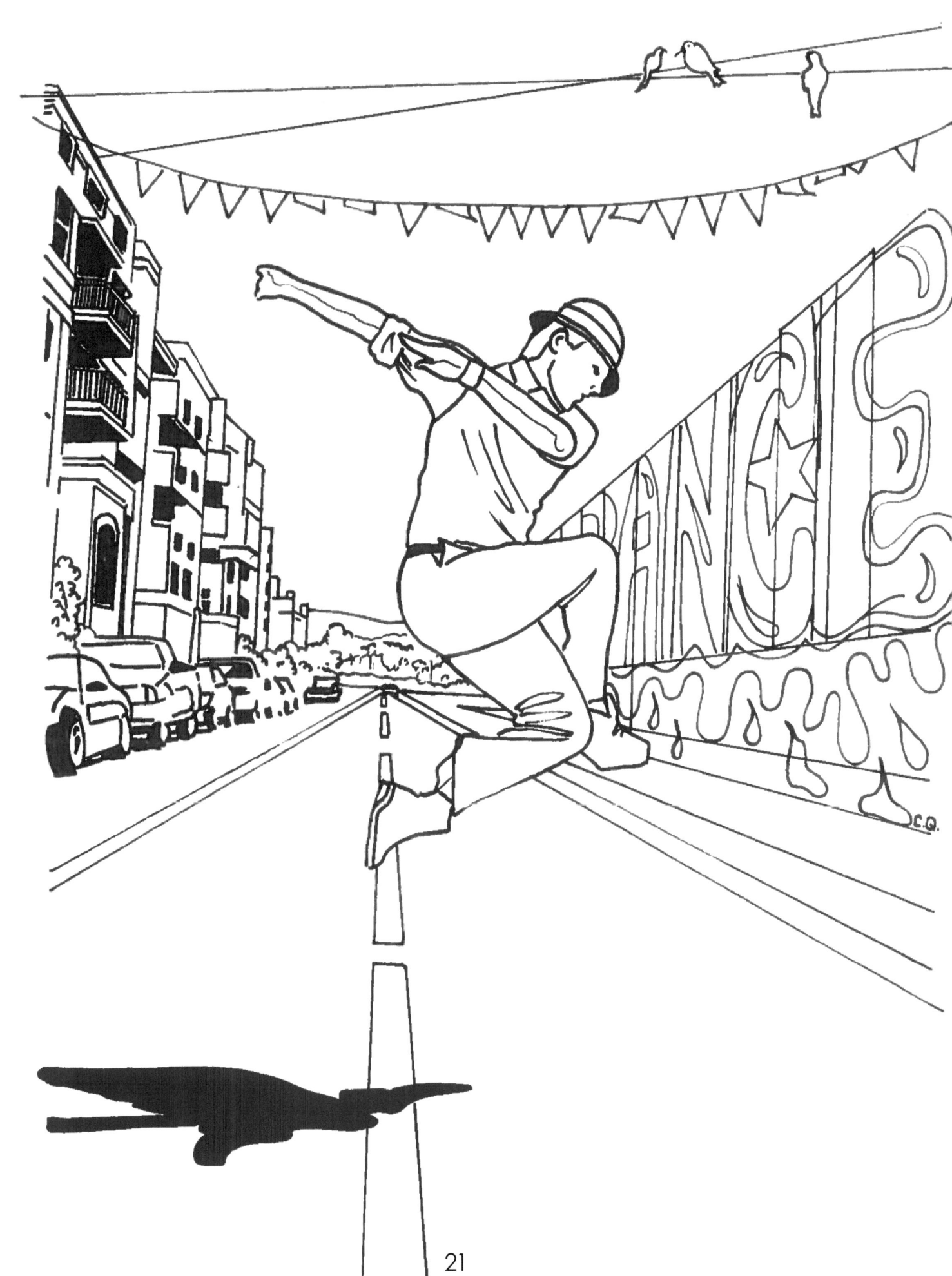